JOCK
JOKES

JOCK JOKES

**Hundreds of Laughs
from the World of Sports**

including

**Baseball ★ Basketball ★ Football
Boxing ★ Golf ★ Hockey
Fishing ★ Hunting ★ Jogging**

Compiled by

Pat Williams

Published by Spectacle Lane Press
Box 34, Georgetown, CT 06829
ISBN 0-930753-17-8

Published simultaneously in the United States and Canada.
Printed in the United States of America.

Introduction

Humor and sports just seem to go together. Perhaps it is because sports contests, so reflective of the human condition, create almost as many downright funny situations as they do dramatic episodes.

In a world where tension is a given, humor is even better than aspirin as a tension-reducer. In a media-dominated age, skilled practitioners disconcert the opposition with well placed barbs and sallies. Humor also serves as a great leveler in sports, cooling anger, tempering the celebrations of triumph, and easing the impact of failure.

In *Instant Replay*, Jerry Kramer, one of the hard-nosed Green Bay Packers, recalls playing for the martinet Vince Lombardi. "Vince had a high threshold of pain. None of my injuries hurt him at all." Humor helped the Packers endure Lombardi's "no pain, no gain" regimen.

Joe Garagiola, Jim Bouton, Jim Brosnan, Bob Uecker, and sportswriters such as Jim Murray are as deft and creative humorists as you will find anywhere, constantly helping to keep events in a rational perspective and highlighting the very human nature of sports and games.

For me, sports and humor have long been inseparable. The rollicking stories of basketball coach Horace "Bones" McKinney shook the auditorium with laughter and made a lasting impression on me as an undergraduate at Wake Forest University. As a minor league catcher for the Miami Marlins I became further converted to the power of the punch line as delivered by a true craftsman, Bill Durney.

Since those early days, I have been involved with over 1,000 sports fetes as a listener and presenter and have had the opportunity to study the masters of sports podium humor.

My short list of the best begins with my front-office mentor, Bill Veeck, who not only was a promotional genius, but was also a marvelous speaker who could electrify an audience with his appropriate use of humor.

I remember hearing my N.B.A. colleague, Frank Layden, for the first time at a banquet and vividly recall how his nonstop humor produced uproarious laughter and a thunderous standing ovation. The rest of my Sports Humor All-Star team includes Garagiola, Lefty Gomez, Lou Holtz, Tom Lasorda, Abe Lemmons, and Uecker.

Jock Jokes brings you hundreds of my favorite sports laughs. Whether you're a spectator, participant, or are looking to score big on the banquet circuit, I know you'll find a lot of lines in this little book that will make you laugh and help you make others laugh and enjoy life all the more.

Pat Williams
Orlando, Florida

TABLE OF CONTENTS

BASEBALL

April is the month for showers and our team's pitching staff is living proof of that.

His team is so bad that if he were sent to the minors, he'd think of it as a promotion.

We named our son "Later" because teams are always trading for a player to be named later.

Our team finished in last place because our batters never got to hit against our pitchers.

My friend said, "I know I'm a loser. I lost my wallet. My wife is very sick. I lost my job. The Phils lost to the Dodgers. It's unbelievable—

leading by three in the eighth and the Phils blew the game!"

A father watched his young son practice baseball in the backyard by throwing the ball up and swinging at it. Time and time again the bat missed contact. The boy noticed his father watching, and said, "Wow, Dad! Aren't I a great pitcher?"

The coach lacked confidence in his pitcher. On the lineup card he penciled in, "Miller and others."

After watching a 450-foot homer disappear out of the stadium, the manager said to the pitcher, "Anything hit that high and far should have a stewardess and an in-flight movie."

It's tough playing in this city. The first time I got into the bullpen car they told me to lock the doors.

The only problem he has in the outfield is with fly balls.

He owes his pitching success to two things: a strong arm and a fast outfield.

After five consecutive hitters nailed the pitcher's first pitch for hits to open the ball game, the manager called the catcher to a mound conference and asked, "What kind of stuff does he have today?"
"How should I know?" said the catcher. "I haven't caught a pitch yet."

I was watching a baseball game on TV and my wife said, "Speaking of high and outside, the grass needs mowing."

Someone asked him why he switched from a 34-ounce bat to a 29-ounce bat. He said, "Well, when I strike out, it's lighter to carry back to the bench."

A Little League coach consoled his team which had just been whipped: "Boys, don't get down on yourselves. You did your best and you shouldn't take the loss personally. Keep you chins up. Besides, your parents should be very proud of you boys. In fact, just as proud as the parents of the girls on the team that beat you."

Manager to player : "Remember all the batting tips, catching tips, and base-running hints I gave you?"
"Sure do, Skip," replied the player.
"Well, forget them. You've just been traded," said the manager.

My kid is going to make it to the big leagues. Already he has a fantastic breaking ball. Just yesterday, with one pitch, he broke a lamp, a window, a mirror, and a vase.

Heckling umpires can be an art form. Three of my favorite put-downs are:
- "Hey, ump, if you follow the white line, you'll find first base."
- "Hey, ump, how can you sleep with all the lights on?"
- "Hey, ump, shake your head, your eyes are stuck!"

No wonder kids are so confused these days. I saw a Little Leaguer being told by his coach, "Hold at third," and his mother was yelling, "Come home this instant!"

Some players have trouble hitting their weight, but he has such a big ego he has trouble hitting his hat size.

I have seen better swings on a condemned playground.

He's been working on a new pitch. It's called a strike.

"Look, Bobby," the coach said, "you know the principles of good sportsmanship. You know the Little League doesn't allow temper tantrums, shouting at the umpire, or abusive language."
"Yes, sir, I understand."
"Good, Bobby. Now, would you please explain that to your mother."

I say let baseball players chew tobacco if they want to. Just don't let them spit.

When a couple arrived at a game at the top of the fifth inning, the woman asked what the score was.
"Nothing-nothing," a fan told her.
"Great," she said "We haven't missed anything!"

You know you've been cut from the team when you arrive in the locker room and the manager snaps, "Hey, man, no visitors allowed!"

I find amusement in small things such as the Phillies' John Kruk doing wind sprints.

He's not known for his defensive prowess. He's made the routine grounder a thing of the past.

I like the good old days of baseball when umpires called the strikes and the players' union didn't.

The pitcher had sensational stuff today. The opposing batters really loved it.

He was once beaned with a pitch. Some say that's the most

wood he ever got on the ball.

We lost 15 games in a row. One day we had a rain out, and the team threw a victory party.

One free agent hit a home run and had his chauffeur drive him around the bases.

He got his start in baseball as a hot dog vendor but was fired when they caught him heating the franks.

Fans in that town love the ballpark Cokes. They contain the best-tasting water in town.

He's not what you'd call a threat at the plate. He's 0 for 75 against the pitching machine.

That free agent doesn't steal bases, he buys them.

You know you're pitching badly when the fifth inning rolls

around and the ground crew is dragging the warning track.

He's such a tough hitter he even gets walks in batting practice.

Our team is so bad we have a "coach boy." That's the kid who goes out and wakes up the coach if one of our runners reaches second.

Coach: "Okay, guys, I want you to line up alphabetically according to height."

Our team was so bad that when they played the National Anthem the flag was at half-mast.

He doesn't have a good sense of the strike zone. He once swung at a ball that the pitcher threw to first trying to pick a runner off.

The team is working on a microwave bullpen to give their relievers faster warm-ups.

The best thing about playing for the Cubs is that you never have to worry about anyone stealing your World Series ring.

I don't like Astroturf. I think baseball fields should be covered like in the old days—with hot dog wrappers and beverage cans.

When I was a Little Leaguer I had trouble putting on my helmet because I couldn't get my ears through those little holes.

I could have been a professional athlete. My problem in baseball was that I could never hit a curve ball. My problem in golf is that I always did.

The only thing that stays in the cellar longer than those losers is a furnace.

A fan yelled to the catcher: "Hey, the only thing that you know about pitching is that you can't hit it!"

I remember when I was a rookie I slid into home in a mighty cloud of dust. Unfortunately, I was coming to bat at the time.

I was a non-violent baseball player. I could go for weeks at a time without hitting anything.

That team lacks offense. They're so bad that yesterday the pitching machine threw a no-hitter against them.

A billboard on the left-field fence read: "Our team uses Arrid Extra-Dry." A fan spraypainted underneath, "And they still stink!"

The team trainer doesn't have to worry about the players getting the flu this year. They can't catch anything.

Our defense is a little weak up the middle. The shortstop is so inept he wears a catcher's mask.

In his job he doesn't come in contact with many people.

He's third base coach for a last-place team.

Baseball will outlast other sports because a diamond is forever.

Why does a million dollar pitcher need relief?

To give you an idea of the kind of season we've had, the person who handled our side of the scoreboard was sick for three weeks and nobody noticed.

We keep losing games, but our team has a T-shirt night, cap night, a bat night. . . How about something exciting this season like a "Winning Night?"

It's not like I enjoy major league baseball that much. I just love cold hot dogs and watered-down soft drinks.

He acts as if he's hit his head on the dugout roof one too many times.

As they say in the opera, " The aria ain't over until the rich guy bats."

I broke my share of windows playing baseball. Unfortunately, I did it when I was pitching.

Umpire: "My eyes aren't bad. I can see the sun and it's 93,000,000 miles away."

He doesn't like people who can't take a joke—like his batting average.

I was pitching a no-hitter and a shutout until the second batter got up.

I was a catcher but I quit. I couldn't stand people looking over my shoulder when I worked.

He was traded for a player to be born later.

His batting stroke is coming around. He's missing the ball

much closer these days.

He's not that quick. When they time him going from first to third they use a calendar.

He's been in the league a really long time. He bought his first wad of tobacco from Sir Walter Raleigh.

What a face that catcher has! I wonder how many games he caught before he bought a mask.

They can't play on grass. They can't play on an artificial surface. They ought to cover the field with paper. This team always looks good on paper.

You know players are overpaid when the manager calls the bullpen and the butler answers.

He put on a lot of weight toward the end of his career. A pitcher "brushed him back" for crowding the plate, and he was in the on-deck circle at the time.

The only player to reach third was our first baseman, and that was because he ran the wrong way on a bunt.

I knew that my career as a pitcher was over when the coach timed my fastball with an egg timer.

That pitcher has doctored so many baseballs he was recently inducted into the American Medical Association.

Their team is so bad they couldn't sweep a series if they hired nine all-pro janitors with corked brooms.

He gets to first base even faster than an ambulance-chasing lawyer gets to the scene of an accident.

He's been in such a slump that when he finally hit the ball through the infield, he had to call the AAA and ask for directions to first base.

Our team is only two players short of being great—Babe Ruth and Sandy Koufax.

We had a tough team. We wore spikes on our feet. Not on our shoes—on our feet!

The state police presented our pitcher with their good citizen award because his fastball didn't exceed 55 mph any time during the season.

The team is so bad they've been eliminated mathematically for the rest of the 1990's.

I wish the baseball season could last longer, but I suppose the players do need a couple of days off to do their Christmas shopping.

Our team was behind by one run in the bottom of the ninth with two out and the bases loaded. I was the leading hitter on the club and was due to bat next. I straightened my cap, knocked the dirt out of my spikes, pounded the plate, straightened my cap once again, hitched up my pants, dug in the spikes, cocked my bat, and then watched the pitcher pick the runner off third to end the game.

Rookie, trying on uniform: "The cap's a little large, sir."

Manager: "Just make sure it stays that way."

The team's manager was not made to feel too secure. The name on his locker was written in pencil.

You know that a baseball player isn't too bright when you see him put on his cap with the visor straight forward and then give it a quarter of a turn to lock it in place.

That team has been in the cellar so long their team insignia is a mushroom.

We score so few runs the grounds crew has planted tomatoes on the third base line.

We're so low in the standings our team plane doesn't even show up on radar.

My high school baseball team had a negative self-image. You know how some teams select an MVP? At the end of the season, our team voted for the LUP—Least Useless Player.

Our coach used to ask, "If we can put a man on the moon, why can't we put a guy on first base?"

Some find their place in the sun and become rich and famous. Others can't even find a baseball in the sun, and they become outfielders for losing teams.

Watching that team play is relaxing. There are no disturbing loud noises, like the sound of a bat hitting the ball.

They've been in the cellar so long their dugout has a sump pump.

Our team would have had a much better season if the strike had lasted longer.

The ump checked the lineup card and no catcher or pitcher was listed.
"Why no pitcher or catcher?" he asked.
"Batteries not included," the manager answered.

My wife just doesn't understand baseball. I said excitedly,
" Look, dear, we've got a man on every base!"
She replied, "Big deal! So does the other team!"

Major leaguer: "I wish the organist wouldn't play that song.
Every time I hear it, I have a bad day."
Teammate: "What tune are you talking about?"
First player: "The National Anthem."

Today's major league salaries are so high it proves that
diamonds are a man's best friend.

Our pitchers are sent to the showers so often the team's soap
budget is up 300 per cent over last season!

He used to play minor league baseball. He realized he
wouldn't make it to the majors when he was traded for a
dollar and a half and a small household appliance to be
named later.

He set the National League record for the most errors by a

second baseman. The commissioner handed him an award for community service, and he dropped that, too.

He hit three homers one season and eighteen the next. A reporter asked him, "What's the difference this year?" He replied, "About fifteen homers."

Wife to husband as he watches the opening game of the baseball season : "I thought they dropped that show last fall!"

I got my son the basic baseball equipment the other day: a glove, a bat, protective headgear, an agent. . .

Our team's shortstop makes the routine groundball obsolete. He can go to his left, go to his right, go deep into the hole...to make errors.

I made a contribution to fighting the disease known as "Garagiola's Syndrome." It strikes baseball announcers and causes them to lose their hair and tell Yogi Berra stories.

The crowd was so small everyone got a foul ball.

A boy came home from Little League practice and told his dad, "I got traded."
His dad consoled, "That's okay, son. Even big leaguers get traded."
"But they traded me for a *glove*!" the boy moaned.

I realized that the chances were high the game would be rained out when I saw three outfielders with fishing poles.

I don't think the new manager is too bright. I overheard him telling the pitching staff to do wind sprints and to pair off in threes.

There's a new product that baseball players are all excited about—tobacco-flavored Gatorade.

He was invited to the old-timers' game and got to throw out the first cane.

When he pitches, he doesn't doctor the ball with foreign substances. What he puts on the ball is made right here in the good old U. S. A.

In the minors, I was hit in the head with a pitched ball. The next morning the headline in the papers read, "Williams' Head X-Ray Reveals Nothing."

"Sure we're behind in the game, guys, but six runs here, and another eight runs there, and we'll be right back in it."

He's a strange ballplayer. Whenever he stole second, he would feel guilty and go back.

He was one of the first managers in the league to use a computer. He fed in all the information, pushed a button, and the read-out said, "Fire the manager." So he immediately pulled the plug.

When the manager benched me I confronted him. "All this talk you give about consistency. Look, I struck out 27 times in a row. You can't be any more consistent than that."

The good news is that even though we lost today, tomorrow is another day. And the bad news is, we've got another game tomorrow.

I wanted to be a big league umpire, but I kept passing the eye exam.

One team is beginning spring training early so that the players can start practicing how to spit.

I wasn't a great Little League player. In fact, the manager penciled me in as a designated out.

It's a good idea that kids in Little League are exposed to umpires that are never wrong and always win arguments. It helps prepare them for marriage.

When I played in Little League, I made three errors in one game and my parents put me on waivers.

The kind of money he's making, he doesn't need to steal third base, he can buy it!

As Yogi used to say, "Ninety percent of this game is half mental."

Talk about dull games. The highlight of the game was a replay of the umpire dusting off home plate.

I was hit in the head with a pitch. The umpire told me to take first base and I had to ask for directions.

Legend has it that Ty Cobb would practice bunting by putting a sweater onto the field until he could bunt the ball into the sweater. My Little League coach used the same technique and had me wearing the sweater.

As a pitcher, I never had much of a fastball. I hurled one, and it fell to the ground halfway between the mound and home plate. I think it collided with a mosquito.

Driving and baseball have this in common: it's the number of times you get home safely that counts.

He's got such a great fastball he could throw it through a car wash without getting a drop of water on it.

He's an uncoordinated player. He went 0 for 3 yesterday, and that was just attempting to shave.

The Allegheny River runs right by Three Rivers Stadium; the way the Pirates have been playing, you can't blame it.

My seats were so high up in the stadium, the guy sitting next to me was holding a harp.

The team complains so much about the umpiring that their dugout is known as the whine cellar.

He says he doesn't attend baseball games because the organ music reminds him of his wedding day.

I still suffer from an old baseball injury I got when a vendor hit me in the head with a bag of peanuts.

He was asked, "How much pressure do you feel going into the World Series?"
He answered, "Thirty-two pounds per square inch at sea level."

Coach to players: "Now refresh my memory. Are you guys still on strike?"

We didn't have a great season. Instead of a highlight film we had a highlight slide.

Fan to an umpire: "I'm praying for a miracle so your sight will be restored."

BASKETBALL

When NBA players win the championship do they feel ten feet tall ?

They're a team in transition. They're going from bad to worse.

We have so many injuries we're considering hiring nurses for cheerleaders.

Which runs longer, the Energizer Bunny or the NBA playoffs?

I wanted to take the family to a Knicks game, but the bank wouldn't approve my loan.

I was known for my famous hook shot. Every time I'd fire one up, the coach gave me the hook.

I've guarded guys that could leap before, but all the others came down.

One of our forwards was so slow that if he ever got caught in the rain he'd rust.

Our point guard is so worn down that when two vultures flew over him the other day, one looked at the other and said, "We're too late. Somebody already beat us to him."

Life is much like basketball: some score points, while others just dribble.

He was a professional bowler before he became a power forward. You should see his alley-hoop play.

One center entered professional boxing after retiring from the league. He's since developed a cauliflower navel.

He looks like a flagpole with hair.

In the off-season, he models for silos.

He also works for the telephone company, holding up telephone wires.

Our center's not very bright. I think he's banged his head on too many doorways.

He's such a versatile player. He can do anything wrong.

Philadelphia fans are so fickle. The other night I heard one of them yell, "Go Sixers. And take the Phillies with you!"

One of our recruits is so fast he can eat ice cream in the rain without having it drip.

Coach after a big loss: "Their players put their pants on the same way our players do. It just takes them longer to pull them up."

He's one of the finest officials money can buy.

He looks like he went to a blood drive and forgot to say when.

Short Player Jokes

He's the shortest player in the league. He's so short he can keep his feet warm just by breathing hard.

It must be tough on him going through life without ever seeing a parade.

He's so short, he wasn't born and raised, he was born and lowered.

He's really generous with his time. He recently did a benefit for "Save the Shrimp."

He won't be playing tonight. He injured himself when he fell off a ladder while he was picking strawberries.

His best sport is the limbo. He's so good he can limbo under a rug.

He got a new advertising contract acting as a spokes-
man for a chain of miniature golf courses.

I would never think of making fun of our point guard's
height. I wouldn't stoop so low.

One fan yelled at our short forward, "Call the cops.
Somebody stole your height!"

I won't say he's overweight, but his stomach crosses midcourt
three steps before he does.

The NBA game is spectacular. You see millionaires running
all over the floor. It's like watching the Senate on C-Span.

The NBA season is so long the players seldom get time to
spend at home with their butlers and chauffeurs.

Our center is a yoga master. He learned yoga trying to fit into airline seats.

I won't say that the playoffs are long, but when they started the season, Reagan was still President.

We have so many injuries the team picture is an X-ray.

His seats are so good that occasionally Jack Nicholson has to tell him to sit down.

He's the oldest player in the NBA. He leads the league in career sweat.

The coach has a run and shoot offense.
If an opponent outruns you, the coach shoots you.

We were the surprise team of last season. We did worse than anybody expected.

The coach is preparing the team for the crowd noise they'll hear during the season. He runs practices with a laugh track.

I don't care how tall they are just as long as their ears pop when they sit down.

We went five and five. We lost five on the road and five at home.

We call him "Accordion Man." He throws so many elbows he could play "Lady of Spain" on your ribs.

He's a disciplined offensive player. If he has the shot, he takes it. If he doesn't have the shot, he takes it.

Our team is so bad the cheerleaders stay home and phone in the cheers.

Our team was known throughout the league for its famous slowbreak.

To succeed in college basketball, recruit in the ghettos, land a seven-foot center, and play only schools with hyphenated names.

Our point guard is a magician with a basketball. He can dribble, pass, and slam dunk. Unfortunately, he can never remember where the gym is.

Our number one draft choice just learned his first three words in French—Coupe de Ville.

He's the kind of player who improves as the season goes along. So the coach told him we had played nine games already.

A winning streak for this team is back-to-back off days.

He had four engineering majors on his team. They didn't win many games, but if anything in the gym broke down, those guys could fix it fast.

I used to believe in the adage, "Practice makes perfect." But it doesn't seem to apply to our team.

He popularized an unusual move called the slam *miss*.

Our team has plenty of shooters. What we need is some *makers*.

One college prospect insists on wearing number twelve because that's what he scored on his college boards.

One of our recruits thought that Sherlock Holmes is a housing project and that Henry Cabot Lodge is a resort in Virginia.

Our latest recruit holds the regional record for six "you know's" over a two-minute span.

Your career should end if when you're driving the lane, they call you for a three-seconds violation.

Our point guard is so quick he can go through a revolving door behind you and come out ahead of you.

The coach asked, "Do you have a uniform?"
"Everything but my shoes," answered the recruit.
"What size do you take?" questioned the coach.
"Fifteen or sixteen," said the player. "But you'd better make it fifteen. I don't want to be too conspicuous."

They drafted a seven-foot center who spent his off-season working as a lifeguard. The guy can't swim, but you should see him wade.

He's a real stiff. He played in the Italian League and they shipped him back to the States. They figured that Italy already had enough statues.

The fellow told his date at the basketball game, "See that forward down there? He'll be our best man this year."
"This is so sudden, Harold!" she exclaimed.

He's musically inclined. He insists on having a mini-cassette installed in his headband so that he can fast break to the sounds of Stevie Wonder.

He is so huge, he wasn't born. He was founded.

He is so tall, his birth certificate reads April 1, 2, and 3.

He tallied 3,000 points in his career. He scored 1,000 and gave up 2,000 on defense.

Coach (after a physical game): "I haven't seen so much pushing and shoving since the day I got on a school bus by mistake."

He describes his job in the front office as being a nervous breakdown with paychecks.

Q. What do basketball players do in the off-season? A. Sit in front of you at the movies.

The referee blew his whistle at us so often in last night's game the pea in his whistle caught fire.

Attendance at last night's game was so slight it looked like it was by invitation only.

My career ended abruptly. My team retired my jersey while I was still in it.

One of our players was so slow the ref threw him out of the game for loitering.

A backup forward on the nation's number one team was asked how he felt about riding the bench. "If you're not playing, you might as well not play for the best."

I always hated when we played games against Ivy League schools. Their pep blocks spelled words I had never even heard of.

I enjoy visiting the players during the Christmas season. It intrigues me to see someone decorate a tree without using a ladder.

We traded for him and he turned the team around. We had a winning record when he came to us.

If the game of basketball hadn't been invented, where would high schools hold their dances?

The coach screamed at his center to get defensive rebounds. "I am," said the center. "It's not my fault they're all going through the net first."

Ivy League coach: "When I ask a recruit how he did on the boards and he answers, 'Oh, about eight a game,' I know that he isn't going to be enrolling here."

He sank three baskets in a row and then made three consecutive turnovers. What a player! He keeps both teams in the game!

Our center never crayoned on walls as a kid, but you should have seen the ceiling!

Coach to assistant: "I had a great dream last night. I met a beautiful blonde on the subway. She invited me to her home, and guess what? She introduced me to her brother who was seven-feet-four!"

We have a guard who has great peripheral vision. He can see the court like a nun in a crowded classroom.

Never play an opponent when you have to look him straight in the belly button.

Our team was really bad. We lost nine straight and then we went into a slump.

A basketball coach bumped into an old lady while leaving the arena. He looked at her and said, "No offense."
The old lady snapped, "You can say that again. And no defense either!"

Coaches who listen to fans wind up sitting next to them.

A seven-foot-three center was approached in an airport by a baggage handler.
"Are you a basketball player?" the man asked.
"No, I'm a jockey for a dinosaur," replied the cager.

BOWLING

Bowling is a sport that should be right down your alley.

If you can't hear a pin drop, then something is definitely wrong with your bowling.

Our small town used to have a bowling alley, but somebody stole the pin.

"Something is wrong with my bowling delivery," Tom said gutturally.

I'll never bowl with him again. After he got a strike, he spiked the ball.

If our town didn't have bowling, there'd be no culture at all.

I go bowling once every four years to make sure I still hate it.

BOXING

He's an ambidextrous fighter. He can get knocked out with either hand.

He was a crossword puzzle boxer. He entered the ring vertical and left horizontal.

I quit because I had a problem with my hands. The refs kept stepping on them.

Ex-boxer: "I'm in great shape. Every artery in my body is hard."

Manager: "How would you like to fight for the crown?"
Boxer: "Great. I think I can take the queen in about three rounds."

When I was a fighter I kept my head. I lost my teeth, but I kept my head.

I know that there will never be women's boxing. A woman wouldn't think of putting on gloves without a purse and shoes to match.

Boxer, after battering opponent unmercifully: "There'll be no rematch for that chump. My hands couldn't stand the punishment."

He boxed as Kid Candle. One blow and he was out.

The boxer had written on his tombstone: "You can stop counting. I'm not getting up."

"My dad is a boxer."
"What is your mother?"
"Extremely cautious!"

His trainer told him to stay down till eight. He looked up from the canvas and said, "What time is it now?"

He only learned to count up to ten. He thought that after ten came, "You're out!"

He boxed under the name of Kid Cousteau because he took so many dives.

The boxer was so far behind in points he had to knock out his opponent just to get a draw.

He's the only boxer in the history of the sport to be knocked out while shadow boxing.

A fighter was taking a terrific beating. When the bell rang, he staggered to his corner. His manager said, "Let him hit you with his left for awhile. Your face is crooked."

"Just think of it," said the boastful boxer to the manager. "Tonight I'll be fighting on TV before millions of people." "Yes," replied the manager, "and they'll all know the results of the fight at least ten seconds before you do."

EXERCISE

His idea of exercise is to sit in the tub, pull the plug, and fight the current.

I've been working out every day this week. My TV remote is broken, and getting up out of the chair 50 times a night is really tough.

The first machine the health club put me on was the respirator.

I enjoy long walks, especially when they're taken by people who annoy me.

Exercise must be good for you. My wife's tongue has never been sick a day in her life.

My wife was forced to quit her aerobics class because she broke a toe. Unfortunately, it wasn't hers.

My idea of exercise is ripping the wrapper off a Tastykake.

I joined an aerobics class for overweight men. We meet in the church basement. Well, actually we were on the first floor when we started last week.

I have a new incentive to do sit-ups. I put M&M's between my toes.

He's into heavy lifting. He carries his lunch to work.

The only exercise he gets is running after the Good Humor truck.

The doctor is really subtle. He suggested that I lend my body to someone who will exercise it.

There's nothing like getting up at 5 a.m, jogging six miles, and then taking an ice-cold shower. There's nothing like it, so I don't do it.

He's developing a more active lifestyle. Now he sits and watches aerobics shows on television.

My exercise club has a relaxed approach. If all the exercise machines are in use, I can wait in the snack bar and have a chocolate sundae until it's my turn.

I really need exercise. I get winded just winding my watch.

I'm not in great shape. I blacked out putting my socks on.

Exercise wouldn't be a problem with me if I had a different body to do it with.

If it weren't for parking lots, some of us wouldn't do any walking at all.

Every time I get an urge to exercise, I sit down with a bag of chips and wait until the urge goes away.

After we do our aerobics, we always check the scales--the Richter Scale, that is.

The doctor said, "Walking is healthier than driving."
I said, "When was the last time you saw a mailman who looked healthier than a truck driver?"

I gave up exercising. I can't stand the noise.

I bought a rowing machine, but I haven't used it yet. I haven't been able to tear the carton open.

My approach to exercise is casual. I enrolled in a correspondence course at the health spa.

I get all the exercise I need these days just by bending down to pick up those blank subscription cards that fall out of magazines.

I did forty laps this afternoon. I ate in a revolving restaurant.

A woman was hit by a truck. In her dying breath, she was heard to say, "Thank goodness. No more aerobics."

How can one believe in survival of the fittest when you look at some of the people running around in jogging shorts?

I asked the instructor at the health club what I could do for my body, and he said, "Schedule it for demolition."

I owe my athletic physique to my wife and clean living. "Clean the car...clean the attic...clean the garage. "

I prefer sit-ups to jumping jacks. At least I get to lie down after each one.

I exercise religiously. I do one sit-up and then I say, "Amen!"

I met a friend jogging in the park. Well, he was jogging and I was sitting on a bench.

I gave up exercising when I broke my nose doing push-ups.

Don't forget, your brain needs exercise, too. Therefore, spend lots of time thinking up excuses for not working out.

Fitness nuts are going to feel really stupid lying in a hospital bed some day dying of nothing.

It's back to school time when all those kids who spent the summer at exclusive camps learning to be rugged, fit and independent, are standing on a corner waiting for the school bus to carry them three blocks to school.

You know that you're out of shape when you can't pull supermarket shopping carts apart.

These days many people get their exercise jumping to conclusions, flying off the handle, dodging responsibilities, bending the rules, running down everything, circulating rumors, passing the buck, stirring up trouble, shooting the bull, digging up dirt, slinging mud, throwing their weight around, beating the system, and pushing their luck.

My figure used to be my fame,
And helped me get ahead,
But that was fifteen years ago,
And now my fame has spread.

When I was younger, I looked forward to getting up early in the morning to exercise. Now, getting out of bed in the morning is my exercise.

Books on exercise are selling by the thousands. And there's a reason for this. It's a lot easier to read than it is to exercise.

His idea of vigorous exercise is to lift his feet while his wife is vacuuming.

This is a big day for me. Today I am taking the training wheels off my Exercycle.

I get enough exercise by stumbling about a mile each day looking for my glasses.

FISHING

He caught a musky that was so big he took a picture of it and the negative weighed five pounds.

"What's the biggest fish you ever caught?"
"The one that measured fourteen inches."
"That's not so big!"
"Between the eyes?"

The water in that river is so polluted that if you catch a trout, he thanks you.

I was glad when one fish got away. There wouldn't have been room in the boat for both of us.

"I caught a twenty pound salmon last week."
"Were there any witnesses?"
"There sure were. If there weren't, it would have been forty pounds."

There are two types of fishermen: those who fish for sport, and those who catch something.

A fisherman was bragging about a monster of a fish he caught. A friend broke in and chided, "Yeah, I saw a picture of that fish and he was all of six inches long." "Yeah," said the proud fisherman, "but after battling for three hours, a fish can lose a lot of weight."

I catch deformed fish. The ones I get always have their heads too close to their tails.

A wife went fishing with her husband. After several hours, she remarked, "I haven't had this much fun since the last time that I cleaned the oven."

"I went fishing and caught a 120-pound bluefish."
Second fisherman: "I was fishing from a boat when my line snagged an old pirate ship. In working my line free, I brought up an old ship's lantern, and the candle was still lit!"
First fisherman, "I'll take a hundred pounds off my bluefish if you blow out that candle!"

FOOTBALL

As John Madden says, "If you see a defensive line with a lot of dirt on their backs, they've had a bad day."

Our linebacker is so strong he can pitch horseshoes while they're still on the horse.

We play in a dome stadium. We always prefer to kick with the air-conditioning at our backs.

Our offensive line was so good that even our backs couldn't get through it.

Football is a game of inches, and that's how some teams move the ball.

I thought one of the linemen had a tattoo on his leg but it turned out to be a government meat inspection stamp.

He's so huge, instead of a number he should have a license plate.

The coach was marching on the field alongside the band. A majorette threw her baton in the air and then dropped it. A fan yelled, "Hey, I see you coach the band, too."

Football is a game when 22 big, strong players run around like crazy for two hours while 50,000 people who really need the exercise sit in the stands and watch them.

Did you hear about the world's dumbest center? They had to stencil on his pants: This End Up. On his shoes they put, T. G. I. F., "Toes go in first."

I say let's make football more entertaining and give the quarterback something else to think about. Let's arm each middle linebacker with a coconut custard pie.

Some chickens were in a yard when a football flew over the fence. A rooster walked by and said, "I'm not complaining, girls, but look at the work they're doing next door!"

The coach says his favorite play is the one where one of our players pitches the ball back to the official after he has scored a touchdown.

The coach was always a step ahead of all opposing coaches. When they started the two-platoon system, he had a three-platoon system—one on offense, one on defense, and one to go to classes.

Our quarterback knows how to do everything with a football except autograph it.

I gave up my hope of being a star halfback the second day of practice. One tackle grabbed my left leg, another grabbed my right leg, and the linebacker looked at me and said, "Make a wish!"

Pro linemen are so huge that it takes just four of them to make a dozen.

Our players have a lot on the ball. Unfortunately, it's never their hands.

He wore number 53. Unfortunately, that was his combined SAT score.

We were in a really tough game. Our quarterback started praying, and we heard a distant voice say, "Please don't include me in this."

That linebacker has rung so many bells he has a fan club consisting entirely of Avon ladies.

We have lots of veterans on this year's squad. Too bad they're all from World War II.

The place kicker missed his attempt at a field goal. He was so angry, he went to kick himself and missed again.

They call it their nickel defense, because that's what it's worth.

Wife to friend:"The most exciting play of the season was when Fred sat on the cheese dip."

I would have played football, but I have an intestinal

problem—no guts.

I knew that he was on steroids. His I.Q. and neck size were the same number.

"I know I told you that I loved you more than football, honey, but that was during the strike."

Wife: "It's Super Monday. Football season is over!"

You know that your coaching job is in trouble when the marching band forms a noose at half-time.

Old quarterbacks never die. They just pass away.

We have so many players on the disabled list the team bus can park in a handicapped space.

This team employs their famous "Doughnut Defense"—the one with the big hole in the middle.

This year I can assure you that we are going to move the ball. I just hope that it's forward.

The only way they can gain yardage is to run their game films backward.

Husband: "Hey, Marie, do you have anything you want to say before the football season starts?"

He retired due to illness and fatigue. The fans were sick and tired of his coaching.

The coach is getting tough. If the team doesn't win this week, he's going to force the players to attend classes.

After the last game the fans tore down the goal posts so our team couldn't play next week.

The Minnesota football coach, commenting on the cold weather: "All the players here have blond hair and blue ears."

Wife: "I read in the paper that a man traded his wife for

season tickets to the Redskins. You'd never do that, would you?"

Husband: "Of course not. The season's half over."

Wife at perfume counter: "What do you have that will compete with three hours of football on TV?"

I once got a letter in football. It was from the coach and it said, "Return your equipment immediately."

The coach put a reserve tackle in for the last ten seconds of a game. "It's a good thing it doesn't take me long to warm-up," said the sub.

The quarterback said of his teammate, "If it wasn't for the huddles, he wouldn't have any social life at all."

We had one player who was so lazy he took a folding chair into the huddle.

Our offensive line was so bad our quarterback started his signal calling by yelling, "Mayday! Mayday!"

Our football team was so bad our homecoming queen ran away from home.

Our team was so bad we had to rent cheerleaders.

After the game, the rookie coach said, "I have nothing to say, and I'll only say it once."

Everyone has fear. Anyone who doesn't have fear belongs in a mental institution or on special teams.

The winless coach was asked if his team prayed before games. "No," said the frustrated coach. "We have so many things to pray for, we'd be penalized for delaying the game."

A football team was stopped at the border in Canada. An inspector asked, "Are you all Americans?"
"No," replied a player, "but we do have an all-conference linebacker."

How can you make a slow halfback fast?
Don't let him eat for a week.

Our offensive line is so bad our quarterback signals for a fair catch on the snap.

To be a successful football coach, you have to be smart enough to understand the game and dumb enough to think it's important.

A coach was asked his prospects for the coming season. "Not so good," he said. "We didn't lose any players from last year's team through graduation."

A man visiting Notre Dame inquired of the football coach, "I understand you have a chaplain on the bench who prays for the team during the game. I'd like to meet him."
"No problem," the coach responded. "Do you want to meet the offensive chaplain, defensive chaplain, or special teams chaplain?"

Our offensive coach works for a bakery in the off season. His specialty is turnovers.

We were a team of losers. We used to hold victory celebrations if we won the coin toss.

Our quarterback is the best I've seen at reading defenses, as long as they're not written.

The coach was asked why he allowed his star running back to carry the football forty times in one game.
"Why not?" replied the coach. "It doesn't weigh that much!"

A football is just a basketball designed by a committee.

As quarterback, he won the Venus de Milo trophy. You know—no arm.

He knew that his playing days were over as a running back when every time he tried to run an end sweep he was penalized for delay of the game.

Coach's pre-game pep talk: "Remember, team, that the other

team is human, too. Unfortunately, they are tremendously huge, speedy, vicious humans."

He has a nagging football injury he got moving his TV set to try to get his favorite team in better field position.

Football combines the worst elements of society—violence and committee meetings.

Q. How many football players does it take to change a light bulb?
A. Only one, but he gets three credits for it.

I asked a University of Nebraska football player what the "N" on the side of his helmet stood for, and he said, "Knowledge."

I played for a really bad team. The quarterback always had trouble giving signals over the noise of the crowd's laughter.

This year his team is going to the Margarine Bowl—that's for the team that can't beat the spread.

"Now go out there and smash them, break their skulls, annihilate them...and now for the team prayer."

In my home, the Super Bowl is anything with snacks in it.

After the Super Bowl, a fan turned off his TV and discovered his wife had left him in November.

We've seen deodorants that offer more protection than our offensive line.

One player to another:"I think I'll start going to class. Where is it?"

I played quarterback for the local business college. Our plays were slow in developing because every time I handed the ball off, I had to get a receipt.

They really have a low confidence quotient. Last Sunday they won the coin toss and elected to *leave*!

They have a player who is an English major with a 3.9 grade

point average. He leads the conference in complete sentences.

The coach asked the athletic director if he would still like him if the team went 0-12 next season.
"Oh, sure, I'd like you just the same," said the athletic director, "but I'd sure miss you around here."

How can you make football jerseys last?
Make the pants first.

The coach berated his team at half-time. They were being beaten 63-7. "We've got better receivers, a better passer, faster backs, tougher linemen. Now, I ask you, 'What have they got that we don't?'"
A sub raised his hand and offered, "Sixty-three points?"

He has a lifetime contract to coach football. That means the college can't fire him in the middle of the game if his team has the ball.

My season seats to my team's games this year were awful. They faced the field.

I'm trying to be more considerate of my wife this year. I asked her whether she wants me to take her out during half-times.

My wife says that she just doesn't understand football. She can't see why 70,000 people would gather in one place for anything except dollar days at K-Mart.

A coach was hung in effigy. He remarked, "I'm just glad it happened in front of the library. I've always stressed academics."

The booster club sent a telegram to the team: "We're behind you one hundred per cent—win or tie."

Asked whether scoring on the first possession gave the team a psychological edge, the coach answered, "Not necessarily. But it always gives you a seven point lead."

A sarcastic sportswriter asked the quarterback whether he majored in basket weaving at the university.
"No, it was too tough, so I majored in journalism," replied the signal caller.

Their football program is very ethical. All they offer their players is tuition, room and board, and $1,500 a week for textbooks, laundry and miscellaneous expenses.

The coach takes all of his recruits into the forest to determine what positions they should play. He tells them to run at top speed. The ones that run straight into trees he makes linemen. The ones who run around them become halfbacks.

Coach: "Okay, Monroe. Go out there and get ferocious."
Monroe: "All right, Coach. What's his number?"

After a frustrating loss, a coach was asked, "What do you think of your team's execution today?"
"Sounds like a good idea," said the coach. "And the sooner the better."

A referee defines the typical fan as "A guy who screams from the bleachers because he thinks you missed a call in the center of the interior line, then after the game can't find his car in the parking lot."

Our team folded so fast last season that they named a lawn chair after it.

We hope to have a great season. The only things we lack now are offense, defense, and teamwork.

In Texas, they only have three sports: high school football, college football, and professional football.

He was a triple-threat quarterback. He threatened to quit the team three times.

The English teacher asked, "Did the coach have someone help you with your term paper?"
"No," replied the player. "He had somebody write it all by himself."

An opposing coach was asked what the nation's number one team did that other teams didn't.
"I've never seen another team kick off so much," was his reply.

I knew our starting quarterback lacked smarts when I heard him call signals: "Two, seven, twenty-four, eleventy-two. . ."

Our school fight song was *The Impossible Dream.*

One linebacker was so huge his number was 52-99—inclusive.

Our athletic budget was really hurting. Before one game, instead of flipping a coin, we had to toss an I.O.U.

Although his team was pitiful, the coach attempted to inspire them. "Look," he said, "if we receive, try your hardest to recover the fumble. And if we kick off, hang in there and try to block their extra point."

One of our tackles was so tough he'd celebrate a victory by eating the game ball.

When I played, the cheerleaders would yell, "Pat, Pat, he's our man. If he can't do it, we're not surprised!"

I was a triple threat. If the coach put me in, my teammates, the cheerleaders, and the fans all threatened to leave.

Our team was so bad that during half-time, the band would march into formation and spell the word HELP.

A linebacker was describing his attributes:"I have speed, strength, agility, and the ability to recognize pain immediately."

The coach screamed at his players: "You should be ashamed of yourselves. For a bunch of college players, you play like amateurs!"

What a thrilling game! The vendors did a big business with hot dogs, ice cream, and No-Doz.

I spent weeks learning the playbook; but it didn't do any good. The groundskeeper forgot to mark those little x's and o's on the field.

He enjoyed playing college football. He told me, " I didn't miss a game, and they didn't miss a payday."

I was assigned to go in and block the referee's view.

A father and son were watching a football game on TV. A quarterback was having a poor game, and the father screamed, "Why don't they take him out?"
His son replied, "Maybe it's his ball."

A dog was sitting at a bar watching a football game in which a notoriously poor team was playing. They kicked a field goal and the dog went into a frenzy. They kicked another and the dog repeated the action.
The bartender said to the owner, "Wow, your dog is some fan. Tell me, what does he do when his team scores a touchdown?"
The owner said, "I don't know. I've only had him for four years."

Q. Why couldn't the quarterback listen to his radio?
A. He couldn't find his receiver.

I wanted to play football, but I had a handicap. I was born with a neck.

Referee: What a football player becomes when he loses his eyesight.

College professors are paid with what's left after the football coach draws his salary.

He was so huge that...

> when he wore a green shirt with white stripes, a gang of kids tried to play football on him.

> he hurts the bathtub.

> the stork couldn't deliver him. They had to use a crane.

> his heart is in the right place, but his stomach hangs down to his knees.

> the airline said it could carry his luggage, but he should take the bus.

his cleats smile when he takes them off.

he's not fat. He's just experiencing a cell surplus.

he's considered to be corporally well-endowed.

A professional football coach is a guy whose job is to predict what will happen on Sunday then explain on Monday why it didn't.

The linebacker says he loves his work because of all the people he runs into.

The coach had the National Anthem played at the beginning of the second half, so he could make sure his players could stand .

GOLF

I play with a golfer who is so accustomed to shaving his score that when he got a hole-in-one he carded a zero.

The world's worst golfer hit a ball into a monstrous bunker. "What club shall I use?" he asked the caddie. "Never mind the club," the caddie answered. "Just take along plenty of food and water."

He asked the caddie, "What do you think of my game?" He said, "It's okay, but I like golf better."

A doctor who golfs has one advantage over the rest of us. Nobody can read his scorecard.

He went golfing with his boss. The boss hit his first drive 50 yards, and it lay 275 yards from the cup, so he conceded the putt .

He's too fat to play. If he places the ball where he can hit it, he can't see it. If he places it where he can see it, he can't hit it.

There are thousands of people who are worse golfers than he is. Of course, they don't play. . .

The golf pro wants me to keep my head down so I can't see him laughing.

"You're so involved with golf," whined the wife, "that you can't even remember the day we were married."
"That's what you think!" countered the husband. "It was the same day I sank a 35-foot putt."

He had to get a new caddie on the ninth hole. He sent the first one back to the clubhouse for laughing too loudly.

The way he plays they should put the flags on the greens at half-mast.

I'm not saying his game is bad, but if he grew tomatoes, they'd come up sliced.

He cut ten strokes off his score. He didn't play the last hole.

The golf pro walked over to two women and asked, "Are you here to learn how to play golf?"
One replied, "My friend is. I learned yesterday."

The position of your hands is very important when playing golf. I use mine to cover up my scorecard.

A Scotsman gave up the game after 25 years. He lost his ball.

I took a golf lesson yesterday, and did really well. In just one lesson I was throwing my clubs as well as guys who have been playing for years!

Rules of Golf

When standing at the first tee, that's as good as you're going to feel all day.

A golfer, like a bowler, can straighten the flight of a ball by yelling at it.

When throwing grass in the air to get wind direction, remember, that the earth is rotating at 1,000 miles per hour.

I hit the ball so deep into the woods I got to meet Bambi.

Shoot his age? He can't even shoot his social security number.

I was three-over today—one over a house, one over a patio, and one over a swimming pool.

I went golfing and lost a brand new ball on the sixth hole. I asked the caddie, " Didn't you watch where it went?"

He said, "Sorry, sir, you caught me by surprise when you hit it on the first swing."

He plays Civil War golf. He goes out in 61 and back in 65.

Golf: A long walk, interspersed with frustration and creative arithmetic.

New book: *How to Line Up Your Fifth Putt.*

A funeral procession passed and two gentlemen noticed a curious thing. A bag of golf clubs was resting on the coffin in the hearse.
"He must have been quite a golfer," said one soberly.
"Must have been? *Is!*" said the other. "He's taking his clubs along to play this afternoon. That's his wife's funeral."

The season is upon us when we golfers must explain to our wives that we're too tired to dig up the garden, but not too tired to dig up the fairway.

He's the only guy I know who putts and yells, "Fore!"

The golfer fell in the lake and started to wave his arms frantically. His caddie said, "I think he wants his eight-wood."

He spends so much time in sand bunkers he carries a beach towel in his golf cart.

Golfers are always complaining. One I know got a hole-in-one and moaned, "Great! Just when I needed the practice!"

The golf pro complimented him on the way he was keeping his head down. Then he discovered he was asleep.

Yesterday I broke 80—on a miniature golf course.

Last time he was out on the links he shot a birdie, an eagle, a moose and a Mason.

I use "Lone Ranger" golf balls. You tee off and they disappear in a cloud of dust.

Confidence? He once got a hole-in-one and said, "Oh, good! Now I don't have to putt!"

He spends a lot of time in the rough. In fact, his favorite club is a wedge with a sickle attached to it.

Golfer: "This is terrible. I've never played this badly before."
Caddie: "Oh, then you have played before?"

A golfer shot a bad round and asked his friend what he should give the caddie.
"Your clubs," said the friend.

With club memberships, the price of golf balls, clubs, green fees, cart rentals, and other accessories, isn't it ironic that golf was invented in Scotland?

He plays a fair game of golf, but only if you watch him.

"Did you drive from the fifteenth tee an hour ago?" an officer asked a golfer.
"Yes, I did," answered the puzzled golfer.
"Well," said the policeman, "your ball sailed out onto the highway and cracked the windshield of a woman's car. She couldn't see where she was going and rammed into a fire truck which was on its way to a fire. As a result, a house burned down. What are you going to do about it?"
The golfer thought a minute, picked up his driver and said, "Well, I'm going to open up my stance a little and move my thumb around farther toward my right side. . ."

Nothing is so discouraging as playing golf with someone who is so good he doesn't have to cheat.

"My doctor says that I can't play golf anymore," lamented a man.
"Oh, then he's seen you play, too?" his partner replied.

Do you like to meet new people? Then just pick up the wrong golf ball.

Golf used to be a rich man's game. Now there are millions of poor players.

One of my goals in life is to get a hole-in-one. And I'm getting there. Just yesterday I got a double-bogey.

Ladies, if your husband comes home with sand in his cuffs and cockleburs on his pants, don't ask him what he shot.

He has benefited from playing golf. His golf game has made him an expert in the field of wilderness survival.

An aging friend said that he's given up trying to shoot his age on the golf course. Now he'll settle for his area code.

He addresses the ball, but not in repeatable language.

He never golfs on Saturday mornings. He hates to miss the cartoons.

I'm a two-handicap golfer. I can't drive and I can't putt.

He spends so much time in the rough, that instead of a golf cart, he uses a Land Rover.

Most people wear golf shoes. He wears hiking boots.

I whacked a ball 350 yards yesterday. Unfortunately I was playing tennis at the time.

Golf is like business. You drive hard to get to the green, and end up in the hole.

I did well on my golf outing yesterday. I got to hit the ball more than anyone else.

Golf doesn't have a fitness incentive in it. The better you get at it, the less exercise you get.

The chief flaw in my game is that I stand too close to the ball after I hit it.

I have two handicaps—my woods and my irons.

My golf game is so bad a sporting goods company insists I not use their clubs.

All afternoon my caddie kept looking at his watch.
I asked, "What time is it?"
He said, "Oh, this isn't a watch. It's a compass."

As if life doesn't have enough heartaches, frustrations, and despair; someone had to go and invent golf!

My caddie is a real pro. He even knew which club to tell me to use when hitting out of a Pizza Hut.

Nothing counts in golf like your opponent.

The doctor told a patient, "You look worn out, Ed. I suggest you lay off golf and spend a few days in your office."

When he's hitting, the safest place to stand is right in the middle of the fairway.

I've been playing for eleven years, and just yesterday the caddie gave me the best golf tip I've ever had. He said I could drive the ball a lot farther if I took the little bag off the end of the club.

I tried to hit the long ball that the commentator talks about on TV, but I found that those round ones work so much better for me.

My 85-year-old friend likes to golf, but he can't see where he hits the ball. So, he takes along his 84-year-old friend, Sam, who can't golf, but his eyesight is perfect.
Bob tees off. "Did you see where the ball went, Sam?"
"Exactly," replies Sam.
"Where is it?" asks Bob.
"I forget," answers Sam.

A golfer was hit by a ball and was lying unconscious in the

middle of the fairway.

As he began to regain consciousness, another player questioned him, "Are you married?"

"No," said the victim. "This is the worst situation I've ever been in."

An optimist is a golfer who assumes that he'll be using the same ball after 18 holes of golf.

Remember, in order to be smart enough to quit golf, you have to be dumb enough to start.

All golfers are entitled to life, liberty, and the pursuit of golf balls.

He always plays golf to relax when he's too tired to mow the lawn.

A golfer is a man who carries 25 pounds of equipment for several miles but has the nerve to call his wife to bring him a glass of iced tea.

The highlight of his day is when he shoots a round of golf so low it matches the numbers on his Social Security check.

A fairway is a well-kept piece of ground that lies between the tee and the putting green. This definition is included because many golfers have never seen a fairway.

Golf balls will last longer if kept in the refrigerator, particularly if they're never taken out.

By the time a golfer can afford to lose a ball, he's too old to hit that far.

One good thing about golf is that it isn't compulsory.

A golfer hit a terrible shot into the lake. He said, "I can't go after that. If I jump in the lake I might drown."
"No chance of that, " replied the caddie. "You can't keep your head down long enough."

He was a cheerleader for the golf team. His job was to walk around going, "Sh-Sh."

The bride-to-be ran up to the groom on the third tee. The groom took a quick glance at her and declared, "I said I'd be there if it rains!"

He knows how to address the ball. Now if he can just put enough postage on it. . .

You can always tell if a speaker is a golfer. He holds the microphone with an interlocking grip.

A golfer looking over a 250-yard hole tells his companion, "I'm going to take this hole in two shots." He tees off and knocks the ball 20 yards. "Now," he continues, "you will witness the longest putt in history."

A golfer requests: "May I play through? I've just received word my wife was in a serious accident.

He slammed the ball into the rough and out flew a quail. His partner quipped, "That's the first time I've ever seen a par-tridge on a par three."

He has a great short game. Unfortunately, it's off the tee.

Last time out he missed a hole-in-one by eleven strokes.

He shoots in the low 70's. If it gets any colder, he refuses to play.

Golfer to partner: "I'm anxious to make this shot. That's my mother-in-law on the clubhouse porch."
Partner: "It's no use. You're 200 yards away. You couldn't possibly hit her from here."

Golf partners were playing the 16th hole when a funeral procession passed. One took off his cap, placed it over his heart for thirty seconds, and resumed his putting stance. "We'd have been married 25 years today," he said.

Golfer: "You must be the worst caddie in world!"
Caddie: "No, sir. That would be too much of a coincidence!"

Teacher: "Remember what happens to boys who use bad language when they play marbles."
Boy: "Yep, teacher, they grow up to play golf."

He does everything first-class. I played with him Tuesday, and he used suede golf balls!

"Why don't you play golf with Bill, anymore?
"Would you play with someone who puts down the wrong score and moves the ball when you're not watching?"
"No."
"Neither will Bill."

My wife ran over my golf clubs with the car yesterday. It's my fault though. I shouldn't have left them on the porch.

He has a golf instruction book that tells him to keep his head down. While he was keeping his head down someone stole his golf cart.

HOCKEY

Hat Day. Ball Day. Hockey teams should have Denture Day.

Hockey is becoming more violent. Last night's game looked like the Mafia on ice.

Reporter to hockey player: "Did you ever break your nose?"
Player: "No, but eleven other players did!"

Hockey players have been complaining about violence for years. It's just that without any teeth, no one can understand them.

They say there are three ways to play hockey: rough, rougher, and "I'll help you find your teeth if you'll help me look for mine."

Hockey players aren't always big, but their bodies are always large enough to hold all the black and blue marks they get in a game.

Our home team wasn't doing well. During a typically horrible game, none of the players had even taken a shot on goal. Finally, one got the puck and a voice from the stands yelled, "Shoot it! The wind's with you!"

The dentist complimented the goalie on his nice, even teeth...one, three, seven, nine, and eleven were missing.

When I was a kid, I thought that hockey players were sent to the penalty box to sit until their fathers came home from work. Come to think of it, that isn't such a bad idea.

Just about the time they seem to be decreasing the amount of violence on TV, the Stanley Cup Playoffs come on ESPN.

Bumper sticker: BE KIND TO ANIMALS. HUG A HOCKEY PLAYER.

A hockey puck is a hard rubber disc that hockey players hit when they are not hitting each other.

(Tom Swifty) "I like hockey," said Tom puckishly.

Hockey is definitely too tough. I mean, what other sport has a coroner.

I've created an invention that will revolutionize hockey and make it the wildest game on earth. It's a clear Lucite puck.

I think hockey is a great game. Of course, I have a son who's a dentist.

In hockey you take a stick and hit either the puck or anyone who has touched the puck.

I knew that it was going to be a wild game when a fight broke out in the middle of the National Anthem.

HORSE RACING

He's really considerate. He put his shirt on a horse that was scratched.

That horse is so slow the post office should buy him.

The next time that horse runs will be from a bottle of glue.

If Paul Revere had ridden this horse, we'd still be under British rule.

Two bookies were coming out of church and one said to the other, "How many times have I told you? It's hallelujah and not Hialeah."

A seven-year-old horse was entered in a big money race which it proceeded to win by seven lengths.
The track manager called the owner and said, "Your horse is seven years old and won by seven lengths. Why haven't you raced him before?"

"We would have," responded the owner, "but we didn't catch up with him until last Tuesday."

My horse was right up there with the winning horse when the race started.

I bought a horse. In its first race it went out 25 to 1. The only problem is that all the other horses left at 12:30.

He's been playing the horses for a long time. As a kid, he was the only one on the merry-go-round with a racing form.

Racetrack: A place where windows clean people.

Roses are red, violets are blue,
Horses that lose are made into glue.

His horse lost the race, and the owner was irate. "I thought I told you to come with a rush at the end," he screamed at the jockey.
"I would have," answered the jockey, "but I didn't want to leave the horse behind."

He bet on a horse that had a photo finish with the truck that watered the track.

It would have been a photo finish, but by the time my horse finished, it was too dark to take a picture.

Horse sense: that innate sense that keeps horses from betting on people.

He bet on a horse that had excellent breeding. After the horse left the starting gate, he turned around to close it behind him.

Before he goes to the track, he always talks to people who know horse flesh—the trainers, the jockey, his butcher.

"Bob, I can't understand how Bill can have so much luck at cards and be so unlucky with horses."
"That's easy," said Bob. "You can't shuffle the horses."

A horse visited a baseball stadium, trotted over to the manager and asked for a tryout. The manager, stunned by the talking horse, figured he'd give the tryout a go.

The horse took batting practice and slammed several pitches out of the park. Next came fielding practice, and he stopped everything at shortstop, and fired the ball to first base each time with amazing accuracy.

The dazed manager said, "Great! Now let's see you run."

The horse said, "Are you kidding? If I could run, I'd be at Churchill Downs."

My horse was so slow that the jockey got paid time-and-a-half for overtime.

My horse would have placed in the race, but he kept looking back for his plow.

I found a way to make a horse stand perfectly still. Place a bet on him.

His horse came in so late the jockey was wearing pajamas.

HUNTING

When he was fined for using last year's hunting license, Zeke claimed, "I was only shooting at the ones I missed last year."

I'll never go moose hunting again. I didn't mind carrying the big gun, but the 200-pound decoy was a real drag.

He bought a hunting jacket with a Velcro closing. He accidentally rubbed up against a moose and got dragged through the woods for five miles.

A hunting foursome paired off. Late at night, one returned dragging an eight-point buck.
"Where's Bill?" inquired the other two.
"He had a heart attack a couple miles back up the trail."
"You mean you left Bill to drag the deer back here?"
"Yeah. It was a tough decision, but I figured that nobody would steal Bill."

A group of hunters fully equipped with rifles, ammo and camping supplies, came upon a young boy armed only with a slingshot.

"What are you hunting for?" asked an older hunter.

"I don't know. I ain't seen it yet," said the boy.

He loves to hunt, but he doesn't own a gun. He just drives the Chevy down to the deer crossing and waits.

A hunter was boring his guests with tales of his safari. Pointing to a tiger rug, he related, "It was either him or me."

"It was a good thing it was the tiger, Bob," said an acquaintance. "You would've made a lousy rug."

First hunter:"We've been here all day and haven't bagged a thing."

Second hunter: "Yeah, let's miss two more each and then head home."

Two men went duck hunting. Five hours passed with no luck. Finally, one of the men said to the other, "Maybe we ought to try throwing the dogs a little bit higher."

A motorist ran over the hunter's favorite coon hound. He went to the hunter's house and told the hunter's wife what happened. She said, "He's out in the field, so you'd better tell him. But break it to him gently. First tell him it was me."

A greenhorn was telling his buddy what a great hunter he was. When they arrived at their cabin, the greenhorn said, "You get the fire started and I'll go shoot us something for supper." After a few minutes, the greenhorn met a grizzly bear. He dropped his gun, headed for the cabin, with the bear in hot pursuit. When he was a few feet away from the cabin, the greenhorn tripped over a log. The bear couldn't stop and skidded through the open cabin door.
The greenhorn got up, slammed the door, and yelled to his friend inside, "You skin that one, and I'll go get us another one!"

JOGGING

I just learned what is on those tapes joggers listen to. "Left foot, right foot."

People from all walks of life enjoy jogging.

You should see him jogging. Yesterday, two worms were chewing on a leaf, and one of them looked up and saw him plodding along in his jogging shorts. He said, "Herman, do you see what I see?"
And the other worm said, "Please—not while I'm eating!"

My doctor informed me that jogging could add years to my life. He's right. I feel fifteen years older already.

A middle-aged runner said, "I don't like to brag, but I've got the body of a 20-year-old."
"Give it back," responded a younger runner. "You're getting it all wrinkled."

I went jogging and was arrested for loitering.

Jogging is a good way to meet new people—orthopedists, podiatrists, cardiologists, ambulance drivers...

I have to admire joggers on a day like this. It takes real courage to show the whole world you're an idiot.

It's embarrassing. I went out for my morning run and a neighbor kid asked me if he could walk along with me.

Frankly, I felt better when I wasn't so healthy.

If all joggers were laid end-to-end, the drive to work would be so much easier.

If speed kills, his jogging should help him live forever.

I was going to jog this weekend, but I strained my back putting on my sneakers.

"My brother has run ten miles a day since he was ten."

"He must be in great shape."
"I don't really know. He's 2,500 miles away."

I belong to "Joggers' Anonymous." When the urge to jog hits me, I call an associate who comes over with a pizza and a chocolate sundae and stays until the urge passes.

"There's nothing like jogging five miles a day and taking a hot shower afterwards."
"How long have you been doing it?"
"I start tomorrow."

Did you notice that people who jog in 90-degree weather are never properly dressed for it? They should be wearing strait jackets!

He jogs each day, five miles or more,
But looks for a parking place near the door.

Jogging is a great way to meet members of the opposite sex, that is, if sweaty girls with calloused feet appeal to you.

I spend my Saturdays sitting on a park bench watching joggers change colors.

He started jogging in the army, only then it was called desertion.

People who run ten miles a day with sore feet, strained muscles, and a burning chest, do it because they say it feels good. Those people will lie about other things, too.

The first time I see a jogger smile I'll consider taking it up.

They say that jogging improves the memory. It's true, too, only I can't seem to remember who told me.

Before resolving to jog five miles a day, visit a cardiologist to have your heart examined, a podiatrist to have your feet examined, and a psychiatrist to have your head examined.

If you think that fishermen are the biggest liars in the world, just ask a jogger how many miles a day he runs.

Marathons do serve a purpose. Running twenty-six miles

keeps all those people from doing something dumber.

A businessman was frantically running around and around in the hotel's revolving door. A bellhop asked him what was wrong.
"Nothing," replied the businessman. "I always jog a mile before breakfast, and this morning I'm expecting an important phone call."

My wife bought me a self-motivation tape that helps me when I'm jogging. It's the sound of six hungry Dobermans barking.

When I jog, I just want to have a stomach that stops when I do.

SKIING

A guy learning to ski remarked, "By the time I learned to stand up, I couldn't sit down."

Then there was the dumb skier who got nasty frostbite on his legs because he couldn't figure out how to get his ski pants over his skis.

Skiing can be a time-consuming sport. I spent one day skiing and seven in the hospital.

Skiing: A winter sport that people learn in several sittings.

All things are possible with the exception of skiing through a revolving door.

I got a useful pamphlet with my new skis. It tells how to convert them into a pair of splints.

I read about a businessman charged with operating a monopoly—three ski lodges and a hospital.

A small girl watching a water-skier said to her father, "That man is so silly. He'll never catch that boat!"

Sign at the foot of a ski slope: Laws of Gravity Strictly Enforced.

Old skiers never die...they just go over the hill.

Ski jumping is where you race down a steep hill and fly 300 feet through the air. There's just got to be a better way to meet nurses.

SOCCER

Soccer is the sport of the future and always will be.

Millions of people play soccer because that way they don't have to watch it on TV.

Soccer players do better academically than football players because soccer players use their heads.

Q.Who are the most indispensable men in international soccer competition? A.The riot police.

A child, playing in a kids' soccer league, was asked by his dad how the game went. He answered, "It would have gone better if the other team would just learn how to share!"

Q. What position did horror film star, the late Vincent Price play on his soccer team? A. Ghoulie.

Q. What has 22 legs and goes, "Crunch, crunch, crunch?"
A. A soccer team eating potato chips.

TENNIS

Anyone who can leap a three-foot net after a match should take up track and field.

We have 750 players in our tennis club. Well, actually there are 50. The other 700 are waiting for a court.

The Bible records the first tennis match in history when Moses served in Pharaoh's court.

Today's tennis pros are so young they give autographs on Etcho-Sketches.

He purposely hits his first serve into the net. He doesn't want to be cheated out of his second shot.

To err is human. To put the blame on someone else is doubles.

A tennis player went to the doctor because he heard music whenever he played. The physician cured him by removing his headband.

Age has no bearing on your tennis game. It just keeps you from winning.

ALL SPORTS

He threw the javelin 200 yards. Actually, he threw it only 100 yards. The guy he hit crawled the other hundred.

Last night on ESPN I watched the "All-Sports Cliché Show." The program featured "on any given Sunday, you've gotta play 'em one at a time, and give 110 per cent, because it ain't over till it's over, winning isn't everything—it's the only thing, that ball had eyes on it, those guys really came to play, they're not going to give up without a fight, no matter who wins, these boys really showed a lot of character out there, and no one can say they didn't have heart."

Rowing has to be the worst sport. You sit down when you're participating and go backward to win.

I said to one of our players, "You smell good. What do you have on?"
He said, "Clean socks."

He had an aversion to physical contact. When he'd dive into the line on a fake, he'd yell, "I don't have it! I don't have it!"

A kid ran cross-country for a college in Texas, and they practiced in prairie land. The coach said, "The only problem with that is, it's so hard to explain to a mother that a coyote got her son."

During a time-out, a ref looked into the stands and saw attendants carrying a woman out on a stretcher. He asked our trainer, "What happened? Heart attack?"

"No," said the trainer. "You called one right and she fainted."

I wasn't much of an athlete in college, but I was waterboy for the swim team.

I've watched so much basketball, football, baseball, and hockey on TV I think I've developed athlete's seat.

When he was playing basketball in college, who will ever forget that magic moment when his teammates lifted him on their shoulders and carried him off the court saying, "And don't come back till the season's over!"

Philadelphia is a great sports town. And the greatest sport of all is competing to find a parking space.

The coach signed a lifetime contract with the university. After two losing seasons, the university president called him into his office and pronounced him dead.

He had so many operations that his knees look like he lost a knife fight with a midget.

My high school basketball team was really bad. Sometimes, to avoid embarrassment, the entire team would foul out in the first quarter.

He's so uncoordinated he couldn't hit the floor if he fell out of bed.

He's non-athletic. He gets whiplash gargling.

He left college early to sign a $26 million contract. There's no telling how much he would have made if he had stayed to graduate with his class.

Coach: The only time my player didn't run up a score was when he took the SAT's.

I was a two-letter man in college—X and O. I was co-captain of the tic-tac-toe team.

Contrary to what he believes, parallel bars are not two taverns across the street from each other.

Q. What's the major difference between a pro athlete and an amateur athlete?
A. The pro athlete gets paid with a check, the amateur with cash.

When it comes right down to it, the hardest thing about learning to rollerblade is the ground.

I was a non-athletic child. My parents had to hire a stunt double for home movies.

Fast? When he's through sprinting, he has to wipe the bugs off his goggles.

Timekeepers at track meets: These are the souls who time

men's tries.

Being a track coach has got to be the easiest job in sports. All you have to say is, "Keep to the left and get back soon."

He was an avid water polo player until his horse drowned.

My wife prefers football to baseball. As she puts it, she only has to watch football once a week.

The trouble with these officials is that they don't care who wins.

He used to be a top athlete—big chest, hard stomach. But that's all behind him now.

This team is hungrier than a starving beaver at a log rolling contest.

I asked him what he runs the mile in and he said, "Shorts and a T-shirt."

His coach gave him a letter in his freshman year, and that letter said that he should try out for the croquet team.

You know you have a green rookie if he signs his autographs in crayon.

Our track team had a cross-eyed discus thrower. He wasn't very good, but he kept the fans on their toes.

If a tie is like kissing your sister, losing is like kissing your mother-in-law with her teeth out.

He's been cut by teams so often he's almost out of blood.

A youngster was explaining to another what the sports term "no-cut contract" means.
"It means," he said, "getting paid your allowance even if you don't clean your room."

Coach after a loss: "I feel like the guy in the javelin competition who won the toss and elected to receive."

Many college athletes are three-letter men:"HUH?"

He gave up his last job due to exhaustion. He was a play-by-play man for ping-pong matches.

What a hypochondriac! He claims he has chess elbow.

The coach said,"You do the high-fives tonight, Williams. Jones, you do the We're No.One's, and that should give Smith his turn to do the Hi, Mom's".

A fan yelled out, "Turn off the lights. Both teams are asleep."
"Leave 'em on!" yelled another fan. "I'm trying to read."

An athlete was asked, "Which record will you treasure most when you retire?"
"Probably the Beatles' *White Album*," he responded.

The doctor told him, "You've got just six months to live. But invest in a losing team's season tickets and it will be the longest six months of your life."

When I went to school, teachers didn't pamper the athletes like they do today. If they wanted to pass, the athletes had to cheat like everyone else.

Coach: "I don't mind turning 50. It's just that at the beginning of the year, I was 43."

To a bench jockey: "Hey, I impersonated you on Hallowe'en, but I strained my back carrying the bench."

He's been coaching the team so long that the word that comes to mind is "institution." Not as a title, but as an address.

Referees have the world's worst job. They get yelled at, ridiculed, insulted, and on top of that, they have to wear those tacky clothes.

You know that your coaching job is in trouble when the booster club gives you a gift certificate from the local U-Haul company.

A coach should have a wife because sooner or later something is going to happen that he can't blame on the officiating.

At half-time an angry coach went up to the ref to complain. "Oh, you're just mad," said the ref, "because we're beating you by ten points."

The swimming coach summed up the season, " We had a semi-successful season. We didn't win any meets, but nobody drowned either."

One coach has moved so often he says, "I've got my furniture trained now so that when I snap my fingers it jumps right into the U-Haul."

He's such a sports nut. He told me that when their first child was born, his wife was in labor for six innings.

His favorite winter sport is watching his wife shovel the snow off the driveway.

I wanted to be a rodeo star, but I just couldn't find a bucking bronco with training wheels.

New York fans would boo a doctor in an operating room.

During the mid-season break, we got the team together for the team picture. And believe me, getting twelve big guys inside one of those little booths at K-Mart is no easy task.

"Bullfighting is the number one sport in Latin America."
"That's revolting!"
"No, that's the number two sport."

I spoke at a meeting of a last place team's fan club. Two of the nicest people I've ever met.

This is the time of the year when general managers look at everything through contract lenses.

That sports announcer's ears are so big he has to use full-figure earphones.

One of our recruits is so fast he can eat ice cream in the rain without having it drip.

I love Sunday games. It's such a welcome relief after fighting the crowds at church.

Chess is not one of your most exciting sports. When you score, there are no cheerleaders to help celebrate. And how do you spike a pawn?

Sign on an equipment room door: "This room is guarded by shotguns two nights a week. You guess which nights."

I asked the hot dog vendor why his hands were all yellow. "People keep telling me to hold the mustard," he said.

I was a great athlete, but bad knees put an end to my career. Before that, I was the best marble player in town.

Sports Laws:

Nothing is ever so bad that it can't be made worse by firing the coach.

The wrong pitcher is the one who's in there now.

A free agent is a contradiction in terms.

Whoever thought up "It's only a game" probably just lost one.

It is always unlucky to be behind at the end of a game.

The trouble with being a good sport is that you have to lose to prove it.

It doesn't matter whether you win or lose until you lose.

In sports teamwork is essential. It enables you to blame someone else.